Anacreon

Moore. 1810.

NRTE

ODES

OF

ANACREON.

VOL. II.

S. Gosnell, Printer, Little Queen Street, London.

ODES

OF

ANACREON,

TRANSLATED INTO ENGLISH VERSE,

WITH

NOTES.

BY

THOMAS MOORE, ESQ.

OF THE MIDDLE TEMPLE.

VOL. II.

EIGHTH EDITION.

LONDON:
PRINTED FOR J. CARPENTER, OLD BOND STREET.
1810.
C. M. H

ODES

OF

ANACREON.

ODE XXXVI.

If hoarded gold possess'd a power
To lengthen life's too fleeting hour,
And purchase from the hand of death
A little span, a moment's breath,

Monsieur Fontenelle has translated this ode, in his dialogue
between Anacreon and Aristotle in the shades, where he be-
stows the prize of wisdom upon the poet.

"The German imitators of it are, Lessing, in his poem
'Gestern Brüder, &c.' Gleim, in the ode 'An den Tod,' and
Schmidt, in der Poet. Blumenl. Gotting. 1783, p. 7." Degen.

How I would love the precious ore!

And every day should swell my store;

That when the Fates would send their minion,

To waft me off on shadowy pinion,

I might some hours of life obtain,

And bribe him back to hell again.

But, since we ne'er can charm away

The mandate of that awful day,

Why do we vainly weep at fate,

And sigh for life's uncertain date?

The light of gold can ne'er illume

The dreary midnight of the tomb!

That when the Fates would send their minion,

To waft me off on shadowy pinion, &c.] The commentators, who are so fond of disputing " de lanâ caprinâ," have been very busy on the authority of the phrase ἢ ἂν Ֆανειν επελθη. The reading of ἢ ἂν Θανατος επελθη, which De Medenbach proposes in his Amœnitates Litterariæ, was already hinted by Le Fevre, who seldom suggests any thing worth notice.

And why should I then pant for treasures?
Mine be the brilliant round of pleasures;
The goblet rich, the board of friends,
Whose flowing souls the goblet blends!
Mine be the nymph, whose form reposes
Seductive on that bed of roses;
And oh! be mine the soul's excess,
Expiring in her warm caress!

The goblet rich, the board of friends,
Whose flowing souls the goblet blends!] This communion of
friendship, which sweetened the bowl of Anacreon, has not
been forgotten by the author of the following scholium, where
the blessings of life are enumerated with proverbial simplicity.
Ὑγιαινειν μεν αριστον ανδρι θνητω. Δευτερον δε, καλον φυην γενεσθαι.
Το τριτον δε, πλυτειν αδολως. Και το τιταρτον, σωνϹαι μετα των
φιλων.

Of mortal blessings here, the first is health,
  And next, those charms by which the eye we move;
The third is wealth, unwounding guiltless wealth,
  And then, an intercourse with those we love!

ODE XXXVII.

'T WAS night, and many a circling bowl
Had deeply warm'd my swimming soul;
As lull'd in slumber I was laid,
Bright visions o'er my fancy play'd!

. **With**

"Compare with this ode the beautiful poem ' der Traum' of
Uz." Degen.

Monsieur Le Fevre, in a note upon this ode, enters into an
elaborate and learned justification of drunkenness; and this
is probably the cause of the severe reprehension, which I believe he suffered for his Anacreon. " Fuit olim fateor (says
he in a note upon Longinus), cum Sapphonem amabam. Sed
ex quo illa me perditissima fœmina pene miserum perdidit cum
sceleratissimo suo congerrone (Anacreontem dico, si nescis,
Lector), noli sperare, &c. &c." He adduces on this ode the
authority of Plato, who allowed ebriety, at the Dionysian
festivals, to men arrived at their fortieth year. He likewise
quotes the following line from Alexis, which he says no one,

who

With virgins, blooming as the dawn,
I seem'd to trace the opening lawn;
Light, on tiptoe bath'd in dew,
We flew, and sported as we flew!
Some ruddy striplings, young and sleek,
With blush of Bacchus on their cheek,
Saw me trip the flowery wild
With dimpled girls, and slily smil'd;
Smil'd indeed with wanton glee,
But, ah! 't was plain they envied me.
And still 1 flew—and now I caught
The panting nymphs, and fondly thought
To kiss—when all my dream of joys,
Dimpled girls and ruddy boys,

All

who is not totally ignorant of the world, can hesitate to confess
the truth of:

Ουδεις φιλοποτης εςιν ανθρωπος κακος.

"No lover of drinking was ever a vicious man."

B 3   —when

All were gone! " Alas !" I said,

Sighing for th' illusions fled,

" Sleep! again my joys restore,

" Oh! let me dream them o'er and o'er !"

———when all my dream of joys,
Dimpled girls and ruddy boys,
All were gone !]   " Nonnus says of Bacchus, almost in the
same words that Anacreon uses,

Εγρομενος δε

Παρθενον ακ' επιχησι, και ηθελεν ανθις ιανειν."

Waking, he lost the phantom's charms,
He found no beauty in his arms;
Again to slumber he essay'd,
Again to clasp the shadowy maid!   Longepierre.

" Sleep! again my joys restore,

" Oh! let me dream them o'er and o'er !"]   Doctor Johnson,
in his preface to Shakespeare, animadverting upon the commentators of that poet, who pretended, in every little coin-
cidence of thought, to detect an imitation of some ancient
poet, alludes in the following words to the line of Anacreon
before us: " I have been told that when Caliban, after a
pleasing dream, says, ' I cried to sleep again,' the author imi-
tates Anacreon, who had, like any other man, the same wish
on the same occasion."

ODE XXXVIII.

Let us drain the nectar'd bowl,
Let us raise the song of soul
To him, the God who loves so well
The nectar'd bowl, the choral swell!
Him, who instructs the sons of earth
To thrid the tangled dance of mirth;
Him, who was nurs'd with infant Love,
And cradled in the Paphian grove;
Him, that the snowy Queen of Charms
Has fondled in her twining arms.

From

"Compare with this beautiful ode the verses of Hagedorn,
lib. v. das Gesellschaftliche; and of Bürger, p. 51, &c. &c."
Degen.

Him, that the snowy Queen of Charms
Has fondled in her twining arms.] Robertellus, upon the epi-
B 4   thalamium

From him that dream of transport flows,
Which sweet intoxication knows ;
. With him, the brow forgets to darkle,
And brilliant graces learn to sparkle.
Behold! my boys a goblet bear,
Whose sunny foam bedews the air.
Where are now the tear, the sigh?
To the winds they fly, they fly!
Grasp the bowl ; in nectar sinking,
Man of sorrow, drown thy thinking!
Oh! can the tears we lend to thought
In life's account avail us aught?
Can we discern, with all our lore,
The path we 're yet to journey o'er ?

thalamium of Catullus, mentions an ingenious derivation of
Cytherea, the name of Venus, ωαρα το κιυθιιν τυσ ιρωτασ,
which seems to hint that " Love's fairy favours are lost, when
not concealed."

                                        No,

No, no! the walk of life is dark;
'T is wine alone can strike a spark!

No, no! the walk of life is dark;
'T is wine alone can strike a spark !]   The brevity of life allows arguments for the voluptuary as well as the moralist. Among many parallel passages which Longepierre has adduced, I shall content myself with this epigram from the Anthologia:

Λωσαμινοι, Προδικη, συκασωμιθα, και τον ακρατον
 Ελκωμιν, κυλικαε μειζονας αραμινοι.
Ραιος ὁ χαροντων ιςι βιος. ειτα τα λοιπα
 Γηρας κωλυσει, και το τελος θανατος.

Of which the following is a loose paraphrase.

Fly, my belov'd, to yonder stream,
We 'll plunge us from the noontide beam;
Then cull the rose's humid bud,
And dip it in our goblet's flood.
Our age of bliss, my nymph, shall fly,
As sweet, though passing as that sigh,
Which seems to whisper o'er your lip,
" Come, while you may, of rapture sip."
For age will steal the rosy form,
And chill the pulse which trembles warm!
And death—alas! that hearts, which thrill
Like yours and mine, should e'er be still!

Then

Then let me quaff the foamy tide,
And through the dance meandering glide;
Let me imbibe the spicy breath
Of odours chaf'd to fragrant death;
Or from the kiss of love inhale
A more voluptuous, richer gale?
To souls that court the phantom Care,
Let him retire and shroud him there;
While we exhaust the nectar'd bowl,
And swell the choral song of soul
To him, the God who loves so well
The nectar'd bowl, the choral swell!

ODE XXXIX.

How I love the festive boy,
Tripping wild the dance of joy!
How I love the mellow sage,
Smiling through the veil of age!
And whene'er this man of years
In the dance of joy appears,
Age is on his temples hung,
But his heart—his heart is young!

Age is on his temples hung,
But his heart—his heart is young] Saint Pavin makes the
same distinction in a sonnet to a young girl :

  Je sais bien que les destinées
  Ont mal compassée nos années,
  Ne regardez que mon amour.

  Peut-être en serez vous emue,
  Il est jeune et n'est que du jour,
  Belle Iris, que je vous ai va.

           Fair

Fair and young, thou bloomest now,
  And I full many a year have told;
But read the heart and not the brow,
  Thou shalt not find my love is old.

My love's a child; and thou canst say
  How much his little age may be,
For he was born the very day
  That first I set my eyes on thee!

ODE XL.

I KNOW that Heaven ordains me here,
To run this mortal life's career;
The scenes which I have journied o'er,
Return no more—alas! no more;
And all the path I 've yet to go,
I neither know nor ask to know.
Then surely, Care, thou canst not twine
Thy fetters round a soul like mine;
No, no! the heart that feels with me,
Can never be a slave to thee!

And

No, no! the heart that feels with me,
Can never be a slave to thee !] Longepierre quotes an epigram
here from the Anthologia, on account of the similarity of a
particular phrase; it is by no means Anacreontic, but has an
interesting

And oh! before the vital thrill,

Which trembles at my heart, is still,.

I 'll gather Joy's luxuriant flowers,

And gild with bliss my fading hours ;.

Bacchus shall bid my winter bloom,

And Venus dance me to the tomb !

interesting simplicity, which induced me to paraphrase it, and
may atone for its intrusion.

Ελπις και συ τυχη μεγα χαιρετε. τον λιμεν' ευρον.

Ουδεν εμοι χ' υμιν. παιζετε τοις μετ' εμε.

At length to Fortune, and to you,
Delusive Hope ! a last adieu.
The charm that once beguil'd is o'er,
And I have reach'd my destin'd shore.
Away, away ! your flattering arts
May now betray some simpler hearts,
And you will smile at their believing,
And they shall weep at your deceiving !

Bacchus shall bid my winter bloom,

And Venus dance me to the tomb!]   The same commentator.
has quoted an epitaph, written upon our poet by Julian, where
he makes him give the precepts of good fellowship even from
the tomb.

Πολλακι

Πολλακι μεν τοδ' σεισα, και εκ τυμβι δε βοησω
Πινετε, πριν ταυτην αμφιβαλησθε κονιν.

This lesson oft in life I sung,
 And from my grave I still shall cry,
" Drink, mortal! drink, while time is young,
 " Ere death has made thee cold as I."

ODE XLI.

WHEN Spring begems the dewy scene,
How sweet to walk the velvet green,
And hear the Zephyr's languid sighs,
As o'er the scented mead he flies!
How sweet to mark the pouting vine,
Ready to fall in tears of wine;
And with the maid, whose every sigh
Is love and bliss, entranc'd to lie

                                        Where

And with the maid, whose every sigh
Is love and bliss, &c.]   Thus Horace:

            Quid habes illius, illius
        Quæ spirabat amores,
        Quæ me surpuerat mihi.   Book iv. Ode 13.

                                        An

Where the imbowering branches meet—
Oh! is not this divinely sweet?

And does there then remain but this,
And hast thou lost each rosy ray
Of her, who breath'd the soul of bliss,
And stole me from myself away!

ODE. XLII.

YES, be the glorious revel mine,
Where humour sparkles from the wine!
Around me, let the youthful choir
Respond to my beguiling lyre;
And while the red cup circles round,
Mingle in soul as well as sound!
Let the bright nymph, with trembling eye,
Beside me all in blushes lie;

And,

The character of Anacreon is here very strikingly depicted. His love of social, harmonized pleasures, is expressed with a warmth, amiable and endearing. Among the epigrams imputed to Anacreon is the following; it is the only one worth translation, and it breathes the same sentiments with this ode:

Ου φιλος, ὁς κρητηρι παρα πλεω οινοποταζων,
Νεικεα και πολεμον δακρυοεντα λεγει.
Αλλ᾽ ὁτις Μουσεων τε, και αγλαα δωρ᾽ Αφροδιτης
Συμμισγων, ερατης μνησκεται ευφροσυνης.

When

And, while she weaves a frontlet fair
Of hyacinth to deck my hair,
Oh! let me snatch her sidelong kisses,
And that shall be my bliss of blisses!
My soul, to festive feeling true,
One pang of envy never knew;
And little has it learn'd to dread
The gall that envy's tongue can shed.
Away—I hate the slanderous dart,
Which steals to wound th' unwary heart;
Aud oh! I hate, with all my soul,
Discordant clamours o'er the bowl,

When to the lip the brimming cup is prest,
  And hearts are all afloat upon the stream;
Then banish from my board th' unpolish'd guest,
  Who makes the feats of war his barbarous theme.
But bring the man, who o'er his goblet wreathes
  The Muse's laurel with the Cyprian flower;
Oh! give me him, whose heart expansive breathes
  All the refinements of the social hour.

c 2

Where

Where every cordial heart should be
Attun'd to peace and harmony.
Come, let us hear the soul of song
Expire the silver harp along;
And through the dance's ringlet move,
With maidens mellowing into love:
Thus simply happy, thus at peace,
Sure such a life should never cease!

ODE XLIII.

WHILE our rosy fillets shed
Blushes o'er each fervid head,
With many a cup and many a smile
The festal moments we beguile.
And while the harp, impassion'd, flings
Tuneful rapture from the strings,

        Some

And while the harp, impassion'd, flings

Tuneful rapture from the strings, &c.] On the barbiton an host of authorities may be collected, which, after all, leave us ignorant of the nature of the instrument. There is scarcely any point upon which we are so totally uninformed as the music of the ancients. The authors * extant upon the subject are, I imagine, little understood; but certainly if one of their moods was a progression by quarter-tones, which we are told was the nature of the enharmonic scale, simplicity was by no means the characteristic of their melody; for this is

   * Collected by Meibomius.

       a nicety

Some airy nymph, with fluent limbs,

Through the dance luxuriant swims,

Waving, in her snowy hand,

The leafy Bacchanalian wand,

Which, as the tripping wanton flies,

Shakes its tresses to her sighs!

A youth the while, with loosen'd hair,

Floating on the listless air,

Sings, to the wild harp's tender tone,

A tale of woes, alas! his own;

And then what nectar in his sigh,

As o'er his lip the murmurs die!

Surely

a nicety of progression, of which modern music is not suscep-
tible.

The invention of the barbiton is, by Athenæus, attributed to
Anacreon. See his fourth book, where it is called το ευρημα το
Ανακρεοντος. Neanthes of Cyzicus, as quoted by Gyraldus,
asserts the same. Vide Chabot. in Horat. on the words "Les-
boum barbiton," in the first ode.

And

Surely never yet has been

So divine, so blest a scene!

Has Cupid left the starry sphere,

To wave his golden tresses here?

Oh

And then, what nectar in his sigh,

As o'er his lip the murmurs die !] Longepierre has quoted here
an epigram from the Anthologia :

Κωρη τις μ' εφιλησε ποθεσσυρα χειλεσιν υγροις.

Νεκταρ εην το φιλημα. το γαρ σομα νεκταρος πνει.

Νυν μεθυω το φιλημα, πολυν τον ερωτα πεπωκως,

Of which the following may give some idea :

The kiss that she left on my lip,

Like a dew-drop shall lingering lie ;

'Twas nectar she gave me to sip,

'Twas nectar I drank in her sigh!

The dew that distill'd in that kiss,

To my soul was voluptuous wine ;

Ever since it is drunk with the bliss,

' And feels a delirium divine !

Has Cupid left the starry sphere,

To wave his golden tresses here ?] The introduction of these
deities to the festival is merely allegorical. Madame Dacier

c 4 thinks

Oh yes! and Venus, queen of wiles,
And Bacchus, shedding rosy smiles,
All, all are here, to hail with me
The genius of festivity!

thinks that the poet describes a masquerade, where these
deities were personated by the company in masks. The translation will conform with either idea.

All, all are here, to hail with me
The genius of festivity!] Κωμος, the deity or genius of
mirth. Philostratus, in the third of his pictures (as all the
annotators have observed), gives a very beautiful description of
this god.

ODE XLIV.

Buds of roses, virgin flowers,
Cull'd from Cupid's balmy bowers,
In the bowl of Bacchus steep,
Till with crimson drops they weep!
Twine the rose, the garland twine,
Every leaf distilling wine ;
Drink and smile, and learn to think
That we were born to smile and drink.

This spirited poem is an eulogy on the rose ; and again, in the fifty-fifth ode, we shall find our author rich in the praises of that flower. In a fragment of Sappho, in the romance of Achilles Tatius, to which Barnes refers us, the rose is very elegantly styled " the eye of flowers ;" and the same poetess, in another fragment, calls the favours of the Muse " the roses of Pieria." See the notes on the fifty-fifth ode.

" Compare with this forty-fourth ode (says the German annotator) the beautiful ode of Uz die Rose."

Rose !

Rose! thou art the sweetest flower
That ever drank the amber shower;
Rose! thou art the fondest child
Of dimpled Spring, the wood-nymph wild!
E'en the Gods, who walk the sky,
Are amorous of thy scented sigh.
Cupid too, in Paphian shades,
His hair with rosy fillet braids,
When with the blushing, naked Graces,
The wanton winding dance he traces:
Then bring me, showers of roses bring,
And shed them round me while I sing;
Great Bacchus! in thy hallow'd shade,
With some celestial, glowing maid,

While

When with the blushing, naked Graces,
The wanton winding dance he traces.] "This sweet idea of
Love dancing with the Graces, is almost peculiar to Anacreon."
Degen.

With some celestial, glowing maid, &c.] The epithet βαθυκολπος,

which

While gales of roses round me rise,
In perfume, sweeten'd by her sighs,
I 'll bill and twine in airy dance,
Commingling soul with every glance!

which he gives to the nymph, is literally " full-bosomed:" if
this was really Anacreon's taste, the heaven of Mahomet would
suit him in every particular. See the Koran, cap. 72.

ODE XLV.

Within this goblet, rich and deep,
I cradle all my woes to sleep.
Why should we breathe the sigh of fear,
Or pour the unavailing tear?
For death will never heed the sigh,
Nor soften at the tearful eye;
And eyes that sparkle, eyes that weep,
Must all alike be seal'd in sleep;
Then let us never vainly stray,
In search of thorns, from pleasure's way;

                    Oh!

Then let us never vainly stray,
In search of thorns, from pleasure's way; &c.] I have thus
endeavoured to convey the meaning of τι δε τον βιον πλανωμαι;
according to Regnier's paraphrase of the line:

               E che

Oh! let us quaff the rosy wave,

Which Bacchus loves, which Bacchus gave;

And in the goblet, rich and deep,

Cradle our crying woes to sleep!

E che val, fuor della strada
Del piacere alma e gradita,
Vaneggiare in questa vita?

ODE XLVI.

SEE the young, the rosy Spring,
Gives to the breeze her spangled wing ;
While virgin Graces, warm with May,
Fling roses o'er her dewy way !

The

The fastidious affectation of some commentators has de-
nounced this ode as spurious. Degen pronounces the four last
lines to be the patch-work of some miserable versificator, and
Brunck condemns the whole ode. It appears to me to be
elegantly graphical ; full of delicate expressions and luxuriant
imagery. The abruptness of ‘Ἴδε πως εαρος φανεντος is striking
and spirited, and has been imitated rather languidly by Horace :

Vides ut alta stet nive candidum
Soracte—

The imperative ιδε is infinitely more impressive, as in
Shakespeare,

But look, the morn, in russet mantle clad,
Walks o'er the dew of yon high eastern hill.

There

The murmuring billows of the deep
Have languish'd into silent sleep ;
And mark ! the flitting sea-birds lave
Their plumes in the reflecting wave ;

While

There is a simple and poetical description of Spring, in Catullus's beautiful farewell to Bithynia. Carm. 44.

Barnes conjectures, in his life of our poet, that this ode
was written after he had returned from Athens, to settle in
his paternal seat at Teos ; there, in a little villa at some dis-
tance from the city, which commanded a view of the Ægean
Sea and the islands, he contemplated the beauties of nature
and enjoyed the felicities of retirement. Vide Barnes, in Anac.
vita, § xxxv. This supposition, however unauthenticated,
forms a pleasant association, which makes the poem more interesting.

Monsieur Chevreau says, that Gregory Nazianzenus has pa-
raphrased somewhere this description of Spring ; I cannot find
it. See Chevreau Œuvres Mèlées.

"Compare with this ode (says Degen) the verses of Hagedorn, book fourth der Frühling, and book fifth der Mai."

While virgin Graces, warm with May,

Fling roses o'er her dewy way.] De Pauw reads, Χαριτες
ροδα βρυουσιν, " the roses display their graces." This is not
uningenious ;

While cranes from hoary winter fly
To flutter in a kinder sky.
Now the genial star of day
Dissolves the murky clouds away;
And cultur'd field, and winding stream,
Are sweetly tissued by his beam.
Now the earth prolific swells
With leafy buds and flowery bells;
Gemming shoots the olive twine,
Clusters ripe festoon the vine;

uningenious; but we lose by it the beauty of the personifi-
cation, to the boldness of which Regnier has objected, very
frivolously.

The murmuring billows of the deep

Have languish'd into silent sleep; &c.] It has been justly
remarked, that the liquid flow of the line αναλυνεται γαληνη ἐν
perfectly expressive of the tranquillity which it describes.

And cultur'd field, and winding stream, &c.] By βροτων εργα,
" the works of men (says Baxter), he means cities, temples,
and towns, which are then illuminated by the beams of the
sun."

All

All along the branches creeping,
Through the velvet foliage peeping,
Little infant fruits we see
Nursing into luxury!

ODE XLVII.

'T is true, my fading years decline,
Yet I can quaff the brimming wine,
As deep as any stripling fair,
Whose cheeks the flush of morning wear;
And if, amidst the wanton crew,
I 'm call'd to wind the dance's clue,
Thou shalt behold this vigorous hand,
Not faltering on the Bacchant's wand,
But brandishing a rosy flask,
The only thyrsus e'er I 'll ask !

Let

But brandishing a rosy flask, &c.] Ασκος was a kind of lea-
thern vessel for wine, very much in use, as should seem by
the proverb ασκος και θυλακος, which was applied to those who
were intemperate in eating and drinking. This proverb is mentioned

Let those who pant for Glory's charms,
Embrace her in the field of arms ;
While my inglorious, placid soul
Breathes not a wish beyond the bowl.
Then fill it high, my ruddy slave,
And bathe me in its honied wave!
For though my fading years decay,
And though my bloom has pass'd away,
Like old Silenus, sire divine,
With blushes borrow'd from my wine,
I 'll wanton 'mid the dancing train,
And live my follies all again!

tioned in some verses quoted by Athenæus, from the Hesione
of Alexis.

The only thyrsus e'er I 'll ask.] Phornutus assigns as a reason
for the consecration of the thyrsus to Bacchus, that inebriety
often renders the support of a stick very necessary.

ODE XLVIII.

WHEN my thirsty soul I steep,
Every sorrow 's lull'd to sleep.
Talk of monarchs! I am then
Richest, happiest, first of men :
Careless o'er my cup I sing,
Fancy makes me more than king;
Gives me wealthy Crœsus' store,
Can I, can I wish for more?
On my velvet couch reclining,
Ivy leaves my brow entwining,

Ivy leaves my brow entwining, &c.] "The ivy was conse-
crated to Bacchus (says Montfaucon), because he formerly lay
hid under that tree, or, as others will have it, because its leaves
resemble those of the vine." Other reasons for its consecration,
and the use of it in garlands at banquets, may be found in
Longepierre, Barnes, &c. &c.

While

While my soul dilates with glee,

What are kings and crowns to me?

If before my feet they lay,

I would spurn them all away!

Arm you, arm you, men of might,

Hasten to the sanguine fight;

Let me, oh my budding vine,

Spill no other blood than thine.

Yonder brimming goblet see,

That alone shall vanquish me.

Oh! I think it sweeter far

To fall in banquet than in war!

Arm you, arm you, men of might,
Hasten to the sanguine fight ;] I have adopted the interpretation of Regnier and others :

Altri segua Marte fero ;

Che sol Bacco è 'l mio conforto.

ODE XLIX.

WHEN Bacchus, Jove's immortal boy,
The rosy harbinger of joy,
Who, with the sunshine of the bowl,
Thaws the winter of our soul;

This, the preceding ode, and a few more of the same character, are merely chansons à boire. Most likely they were
the effusions of the moment of conviviality, and were sung, we
imagine, with rapture in Greece; but that interesting association, by which they always recalled the convivial emotions that
produced them, can be very little felt by the most enthusiastic
reader; and much less by a phlegmatic grammarian, who sees
nothing in them but dialects and particles.

Who, with the sunshine of the bowl,

Thaws the winter of our soul; &c.] Αυαιος is the title which
he gives to Bacchus in the original. It is a curious circumstance, that Plutarch mistook the name of Levi among the
Jews for Λιυ. (one of the bacchanal cries), and accordingly
supposed that they worshipped Bacchus.

When

When to my inmost core he glides,
And bathes it with his ruby tides,
A flow of joy, a lively heat,
Fires my brain, and wings my feet;
'T is surely something sweet, I think,
Nay, something heavenly sweet, to drink!
Sing, sing of love, let music's breath
Softly beguile our rapturous death,
While, my young Venus, thou and I
To the voluptuous cadence die!
Then waking from our languid trance,
Again we 'll sport, again we 'll dance.

ODE L.

WHEN I drink, I feel, I feel,
Visions of poetic zeal!
Warm with the goblet's fresh'ning dews,
My heart invokes the heavenly Muse.

When

Faber thinks this spurious; but, I believe, he is singular in
his opinion. It has all the spirit of our author. Like the
wreath which he presented in the dream, "it smells of Anacreon."

The form of this ode, in the original, is remarkable. It is
a kind of song of seven quatrain stanzas, each beginning with
the line

'Οτ' εγω πιω τον οινον.

The first stanza alone is incomplete, consisting but of three
lines.

"Compare with this poem (says Degen) the verses of
Hagedorn, lib. v. der Wein, where that divine poet has wan-
.toned in the praises of wine."

When I drink, I feel, I feel,

Visions of poetic zeal] "Anacreon is not the only one (says
Longepierre),

When I drink, my sorrow 's o'er ;
I think of doubts and fears no more ;
But scatter to the railing wind
Each gloomy phantom of the mind !
When I drink, the jesting boy
Bacchus himself partakes my joy ;
And while we dance through breathing bowers,
Whose every gale is rich with flowers,

In

Longepierre), whom wine has inspired with poetry. There is
an epigram in the first book of the Anthologia, which begins
thus :

> Οινος τοι χαριντι μεγας πιλαι ἱππος αοιδω,
> 'Υδωρ δι πινων, καλον ἡ τιχοις ιπος."

If with water you fill up your glasses,
    You 'll never write any thing wise ;
For wine is the horse of Parnassus,
    Which hurries a bard to the skies !

And while we dance through breathing bowers, &c.] If some
of the translators had observed Doctor Trapp's caution, with
regard to πολυανθισιν μ' εν αυραις, "Cave ne cœlum intelligas,"
they would not have spoiled the simplicity of Anacreon's
                                                      fancy,

In bowls he makes my senses swim,

Till the gale breathes of nought but him!

When I drink, I deftly twine

Flowers, begem'd with tears of wine;

And, while with festive hand I spread

The smiling garland round my head,

Something whispers in my breast,

How sweet it is to live at rest!

When I drink, and perfume stills

Around me all in balmy rills,

fancy, by such extravagant conceptions of the passage.   Could
our poet imagine such bombast as the following ?

> Quand je bois, mon œil s'imagine
> Que, dans un tourbillon plein de parfums divers,
> Bacchus m' importe dans les airs,
> Rempli de sa liqueur divine.

Or this :

> Indi mi mena
> Mentre lietro ebro deliro,
> Bacco in giro
> Per la vaga aura serena.

Then

Then as some beauty, smiling roses,

In languor on my breast reposes,

Venus! I breathe my vows to thee,

In many a sigh of luxury!

When I drink, my heart refines,

And rises as the cup declines;

Rises in the genial flow,

That none but social spirits know,

When youthful revellers, round the bowl,

Dilating, mingle soul with soul!

                                        When

When youthful revellers, round the bowl,

Dilating, mingle soul with soul!] Subjoined to Gail's edition
of Anacreon, there are some curious letters upon the Θιασοι of
the ancients, which appeared in the French Journals. At the
opening of the Odeon in Paris, the managers of the spectacle
requested Professor Gail to give them some uncommon name
for the fêtes of this institution. He suggested the word
" Thiase," which was adopted; but the literati of Paris
questioned the propriety of it, and addressed their criticisms

When I drink, the bliss is mine ;
There 's bliss in every drop of wine !
All other joys that I have known,
I 've scarcely dar'd to call my own;
But this the Fates can ne'er destroy, -
Till death o'ershadows all my joy !

to Gail through the medium of the public prints. Two or
three of the letters he has inserted in his edition, and they have
elicited from him some learned research on the subject.

ODE LI.

FLY not thus my brow of snow,
Lovely wanton! fly not so.
Though the wane of age is mine,
Though the brilliant flush is thine,

Still

Alberti has imitated this ode; and Capilupus, in the following epigram, has given a version of it:

Cur, Lalage, mea vita, meos contemnis amores?
Cur fugis e nostro pulchra puella sinu?
Ne fugias, sint sparsa licet mea tempora canis,
Inque tuo roseus fulgeat ore color.
Aspice ut intextas deceant quoque flore corollas
Candida purpureis lilia mista rosis.

Oh! why repel my soul's impassion'd vow,
And fly, beloved maid, these longing arms?
Is it, that wintry time has strew'd my brow,
And thine are all the summer's roseate charms?

See

Still I'm doom'd to sigh for thee,

Blest, if thou couldst sigh for me!

See, in yonder flowery braid,

Cull'd for thee, my blushing maid,

How the rose, of orient glow,

Mingles with the lily's snow;

Mark, how sweet their tints agree,

Just, my girl, like thee and me!

See the rich garlands, cull'd in vernal weather,
  Where the young rosebud with the lily glows,
  In wreaths of love we thus may twine together,
  And I will be the lily, thou the rose.

See, in yonder flowery braid,
Cull'd for thee, my blushing maid.] In the same manner
that Anacreon pleads for the whiteness of his locks, from the
beauty of the colour in garlands, a shepherd, in Theocritus,
endeavours to recommend his black hair:

Και το ιον μελαν εστι, και ά γραπτα υακινθος
Αλλ᾽ εμπας εν τοις στεφανοις τα πρωτα λεγονται.

Longepierre, Barnes, &c.

ODE LII.

Away, away, you men of rules,
What have I to do with schools?
They 'd make me learn, they 'd make me think,
But would they make me love and drink?

"This is doubtless the work of a more modern poet than
Anacreon: for at the period when he lived rhetoricians were
not known." Degen.

Though the antiquity of this ode is confirmed by the Vatican
manuscript, I am very much inclined to agree in this argu-
ment against its authenticity; for though the dawnings of
rhetoric might already have appeared, the first who gave it
any celebrity, was Corax of Syracuse, and he flourished in the
century after Anacreon.

Our poet anticipated the ideas of Epicurus, in his aversion
to the labours of learning, as well as his devotion to volup-
tuousness. Πασαν παιδειαν μακαριε φευγε, said the philosopher of the garden in a letter to Pythocles.

Teach

Teach me this; and let me swim
My soul upon the goblet's brim ;
Teach me this, and let me twine
My arms around the nymph divine !
Age begins to blanch my brow,
I 've time for nought but pleasure now.
Fly, and cool my goblet's glow
At yonder fountain's gelid flow ;

Teach me this, and let me twine
My arms around the nymph divine !] By χρυσης Αφροδιτης here, I understand some beautiful girl, in the same manner that Λυαιος is often used for wine. " Golden" is frequently an epithet of beauty. Thus in Virgil, " Venus aurea ;" and in Propertius, " Cynthia aurea." Tibullus, however, calls an old woman, " golden."

The translation d'Autori Anonimi, as usual, wantons on this passage of Anacreon :

> E m' insegni con piu rare
> Forme accorte d' involare
> Ad amabile beltade
> Il bel-cinto d' onestade.

I 'll

I 'll quaff, my boy, and calmly sink
This soul to slumber as I drink!
Soon, too soon, my jocund slave,
You 'll deck your master's grassy grave;
And there 's an end—for ah! you know
They drink but little wine below!

And there's an end—for ah! you know
They drink but little wine below!]   Thus the witty Mainard:

La Mort nous guette; et quand ses lois
Nous ont enfermés une fois
Au sein d'une fosse profonde,
Adieu bons vins et bon repas,
Ma science ne trouve pas
Des cabarets en l'autre monde.

From Mainard, Gombauld, and De Cailly, old French poets,
some of the best epigrams of the English language are borrowed.

ODE LIII.

Wʜᴇɴ I behold the festive train
Of dancing youth, I'm young again!
Memory wakes her magic trance,
And wings me lightly through the dance.
"Come, Cybeba, smiling maid!
Cull the flower and twine the braid;
Bid the blush of summer's rose
Burn upon my brow of snows;

And

___

Bid the blush of summer's rose
Burn upon my brow of snows; &c.] Licetus, in his Hiero-
glyphica, quoting two of our poet's odes, where he calls for
garlands, remarks, "Constat igitur floreas coronas poetis et
potantibus in symposio convenire, non autem sapientibus et
philosophiam affectantibus."—" It appears that wreaths of
flowers were adapted for poets and revellers at banquets, but
by no means became those who had pretensions to wisdom and
philosophy."

And let me, while the wild and young

Trip the hoary dance along,

Fling my heap of years away,

And be as wild, as young as they.

Hither haste, some cordial soul!

Give my lips the brimming bowl;

Oh! you will see this hoary sage

Forget his locks, forget his age.

He still can chant the festive hymn,

He still can kiss the goblet's brim;

He

philosophy." On this principle, in his 152d chapter, he discovers a refinement in Virgil, describing the garland of the poet Silenus, as fallen off; which distinguishes, he thinks, the divine intoxication of Silenus from that of common drunkards, who always wear their crowns while they drink. This, indeed, is the " labor ineptiarum" of commentators.

He still can kiss the goblet's brim; &c.] Wine is prescribed by Galen, as an excellent medicine for old men: " Quod frigidos et humoribus expletos calefaciat, &c.;" but Nature was Anacreon's physician.

E 2   There

He still can act the mellow raver,

And play the fool as sweet as ever!

There is a proverb in Eriphus, as quoted by Athenæus, which says, " that wine makes an old man dance, whether he will or not."

Λογος ες' αρχαιος, ε κακως εχων,
Οινον λεγυσι τας γεροντας, ε ωστερ
Πλεθων χορειν ε θελοντας.

ODE LIV.

METHINKS, the pictur'd bull we see
Is amorous Jove—it must be he!
How fondly blest he seems to bear
That fairest of Phoenician fair!

" This ode is written upon a picture which represented the
rape of Europa." Madame Dacier.

It may perhaps be considered as a description of one of those
coins, which the Sidonians struck off in honour of Europa, re-
presenting a woman carried across the sea by a bull. Thus
Natalis Comes, lib. viii. cap. 23. " Sidonii numismata cum
foeminâ tauri dorso insidente ac mare transfretante, cuderunt
in ejus honorem." In the little treatise upon the goddess of
Syria, attributed very falsely to Lucian, there is mention of this
coin, and of a temple dedicated by the Sidonians to Astarte,
whom some, it appears, confounded with Europa.

Moschus has written a very beautiful idyll on the story of
Europa.

E 3   How

How proud he breasts the foamy tide,
And spurns the billowy surge aside!
Could any beast of vulgar vein,
Undaunted thus defy the main?
No: he descends from climes above,
He looks the God, he breathes of Jove!

No: he descends from climes above,
He looks the God, he breathes of Jove!]   Thus Moschus:

Κρυψε θεον και τρεψε δεμας· και γινετο ταυρος.

The God forgot himself, his heaven, for love,
And a bull's form belied th' almighty Jove.

ODE LV.

WHILE we invoke the wreathed spring,
Resplendent rose ! to thee we'll sing ;
Resplendent rose, the flower of flowers,
Whose breath perfumes Olympus' bowers;

Whose

This ode is a brilliant panegyric on the rose. "All antiquity, (says Barnes) has produced nothing more beautiful."

From the idea of peculiar excellence, which the ancients attached to this flower, arose a pretty proverbial expression, used by Aristophanes, according to Suidas, ροδα μ'ειρηκας, "You have spoken roses," a phrase somewhat similar to the "dire des fleurettes" of the French. In the same idea of excellence originated, I doubt not, a very curious application of the word ροδον, for which the inquisitive reader may consult Gaulminus upon the epithalamium of our poet, where it is introduced in the romance of Theodorus. Muretus, in one of his elegies, calls his mistress his rose :

Jam te igitur rursus teneo, formosula, jam te
(Quid trepidas ?) teneo ; jam, rosa, te teneo. Eleg. 8.

E 4

Now

Whose virgin blush, of chasten'd dye,

Enchants so much our mortal eye.

When pleasure's bloomy season glows,

The Graces love to twine the rose;

Now I again embrace thee, dearest,
(Tell me, wanton, why thou fearest?)
Again my longing arms infold thee,
Again, my rose, again I hold thee.

This, like most of the terms of endearment in the modern
Latin poets, is taken from Plautus; they were vulgar and col-
loquial in his time, and they are among the elegancies of the
modern Latinists.

Passeratius alludes to the ode before us, in the beginning of
his poem on the Rose:

Carmine digna rosa est; vellem caneretur ut illam
Teius argutâ cecinit testudine vates.

Resplendent rose! to thee we'll sing;] I have passed over the
line συν ἱταιρις αυξει μελαιην; it is corrupt in this original reading, and has been very little improved by the annotators. I
should suppose it to be an interpolation, if it were not for a line
which occurs afterwards: φερε δη φυσιν λιγωμιν.

The

The rose is warm Dione's bliss,
And flushes like Dione's kiss!
Oft has the poet's magic tongue
The rose's fair luxuriance sung;

              And

The rose is warm Dione's bliss, &c.] Belleau, in a note upon an old French poet, quoting the original here αφροδισιαν τ'αθυρμα, translates it, " comme les délices et mignardises de Venus."

Oft has the poet's magic tongue
The rose's fair luxuriance sung; &c.] The following is a fragment of the Lesbian poetess. It is cited in the romance of Achilles Tatius, who appears to have resolved the numbers into prose. Ει τοις ανθεσιν ηθελεν ὁ Ζευς επιθειναι βασιλεα, το ῥοδον αν των ανθεων εβασιλευε. γης εςι κοσμος, φυτων αγλαισμα, οφθαλμος ανθεων; λειμωνος ερυθημα, καλλος αςραπτον. Ερωτος πνει, Αφροδιτην προξενει, ευωδεσι φυλλοις κομᾶ, ευκινητοις πεταλοις τρυφᾶ. το πεταλον το Ζεφυρω γελᾶ.

    If Jove would give the leafy bowers
    A queen for all their world of flowers,
    The rose would be the choice of Jove,
    And blush, the queen of every grove.
    Sweetest child of weeping morning,
    Gem, the vest of earth adorning,

              Eye

And long the Muses, heavenly maids,
Have rear'd it in their tuneful shades.
When, at the early glance of morn,
It sleeps upon the glittering thorn,
'T is sweet to dare the tangled fence,
To cull the timid flowret thence,
And wipe with tender hand away
The tear that on its blushes lay!
'T is sweet to hold the infant stems,
Yet dropping with Aurora's gems,
And fresh inhale the spicy sighs
That from the weeping buds arise.

Eye of flowrets, glow of lawns,
Bud of beauty nurs'd by dawns:
Soft the soul of love it breathes,
Cypria's brow with magic wreaths,
And, to the Zephyr's warm caresses,
Diffuses all its verdant tresses,
Till, glowing with the wanton's play,
It blushes a diviner hay!

When

When revel reigns, when mirth is high,
And Bacchus beams in every eye,
Our rosy fillets scent exhale,
And fill with balm the fainting gale!
Oh! there is nought in nature bright,
Where roses do not shed their light!
When morning paints the orient skies,
Her fingers burn with roseate dies;
The nymphs display the rose's charms,
It mantles o'er their graceful arms;
Through Cytherea's form it glows,
And mingles with the living snows.

When morning paints the orient skies,
Her fingers burn with roseate dies; &c.] In the original here,
he enumerates the many epithets of beauty, borrowed from
roses, which were used by the poets, παρα των σοφων. We see
that poets were dignified in Greece with the title of sages: even
the careless Anacreon, who lived but for love and voluptuous-
ness, was called by Plato the wise Anacreon. Fuit hæc sa-
pientia quondam.

                                        The

The rose distils a healing balm,
The beating pulse of pain to calm;
Preserves the cold inurned clay,
And mocks the vestige of decay. :

And

Preserves the cold inurned clay, &c.] He here alludes to the
use of the rose in embalming; and, perhaps (as Barnes thinks),
to the rosy unguent with which Venus anointed the corpse of
Hector. Homer's Iliad ψ. It may likewise regard the ancient
practice of putting garlands of roses on the dead, as in Statius,
Theb. lib. x. 782.

———hi sertis, hi veris honore soluto
Accumulant artus patriâque in sede reponunt
Corpus odoratum.

Where "veris honor," though it mean every kind of flowers,
may seem more particularly to refer to the rose, which our
poet in another ode calls ιαρος μηλημα. We read, in the
Hieroglyphics of Pierius, lib. lv. that some of the ancients used
to order in their wills, that roses should be annually scattered
on their tombs, and he has adduced some sepulchral inscrip-
tions to this purpose.

And mocks the vestige of decay.] When he says that this
flower prevails over time itself, he still alludes to its efficacy
in embalment (tenerâ poneret ossa rosâ. Propert. lib. i. eleg.
17), or perhaps to the subsequent idea of its fragrance surviv-
ing

And, when at length, in pale decline,
Its florid beauties fade and pine,
Sweet as in youth, its balmy breath
Diffuses odour e'en in death!
Oh! whence could such a plant have sprung?
Attend—for thus the tale is sung.

ing its beauty; for he can scarcely mean to praise for duration
the "nimium breves flores" of the rose. Philostratus com-
pares this flower with love, and says, that they both defy the
influence of time; χρόνον δε ουτε Ερως, ουτε ροδα οιδεν. Unfor-
tunately the similitude lies not in their duration, but their
transience.

Sweet as in youth, its balmy breath
Diffuses odour e'en in death !] Thus Caspar Barlæus, in his
Ritus Nuptiarum:

Ambrosium late rosa tunc quoque spargit odorem,
Cum fluit, aut multo languida sole jacet.

Nor then the rose its odour loses,
When all its flushing beauties die ;
Nor less ambrosia balm diffuses,
When wither'd by the solar eye!

When,

When, humid, from the silvery stream,
Effusing beauty's warmest beam,
Venus appear'd, in flushing hues,
Mellow'd by ocean's briny dews ;
When, in the starry courts above,
The pregnant brain of mighty Jove
Disclos'd the nymph of azure glance,
The nymph who shakes the martial lance !
Then, then, in strange eventful hour,
The earth produc'd an infant flower,
Which sprung, with blushing tinctures drest,
And wanton'd o'er its parent breast.
The gods beheld this brilliant birth,
And hail'd the Rose, the boon of earth!
With nectar drops, a ruby tide,
The sweetly orient buds they dyed,

                      And

With nectar drops, a ruby tide,
The sweetly orient buds they dyed, &c.] The author of the
                          " Pervigilium

And bade them bloom, the flowers divine
Of him who sheds the teeming vine ;
And bade them on the spangled thorn
Expand their bosoms to the morn.

"Pervigilium Veneris" (a poem attributed to Catullus, the style of which appears to me to have all the laboured luxuriance of a much later period) ascribes the tincture of the rose to the blood from the wound of Adonis—

————rosæ
Fuse aprino de cruore——

according to the emendation of Lipsius. In the following epigram this hue is differently accounted for:

Illa quidem studiosa suum defendere Adonim,
　Gradivus stricto quem petit ense ferox,
Affixit duris vestigia cæca rosetis,
　Albaque divino picta cruore rosa est.

While the enamour'd queen of joy
　Flies to protect her lovely boy,
　On whom the jealous war-god rushes;
She treads upon a thorned rose,
　And while the wound with crimson flows,
　The snowy flowret feels her blood, and blushes!

ODE LVI.

He, who instructs the youthful crew
To bathe them in the brimmer's dew,
And taste, uncloy'd by rich excesses,
All the bliss that wine possesses!
He, who inspires the youth to glance
In winged circlets through the dance;
Bacchus, the god again is here,
And leads along the blushing year;

"Compare with this elegant ode the verses of Uz, lib. i. die Weinlese." Degen.

This appears to be one of the hymns which were sung at the anniversary festival of the vintage; one of the επιληνιοι ὑμνοι, as our poet himself terms them in the fifty-ninth ode. We cannot help feeling a peculiar veneration for these relics of the religion of antiquity. Horace may be supposed to have written the nineteenth ode of his second book, and the twenty-fifth of the third, for some bacchanalian celebration of this kind.

The

The blushing year with rapture teems,
Ready to shed those cordial streams,
Which, sparkling in the cup of mirth,
Illuminate the sons of earth !
And when the ripe and vermil wine,
Sweet infant of the pregnant vine,
Which now in mellow clusters swells,
Oh ! when it bursts its rosy cells,
The heavenly stream shall mantling flow,
To balsam every mortal woe !

Which, sparkling in the cup of mirth,
Illuminate the sons of earth !] In the original ωοτον αςοτον κομιζων. Madame Dacier thinks that the poet here had the nepenthé of Homer in his mind. Odyssey, lib. iv. This nepenthé was a something of exquisite charm, infused by Helen into the wine of her guests, which had the power of dispelling every anxiety. A French writer, with very elegant gallantry, conjectures that this spell, which made the bowl so beguiling, was the charm of Helen's conversation. See De Meré, quoted by Bayle, art. Hélène.

No youth shall then be wan or weak,
For dimpling health shall light the cheek;
No heart shall then desponding sigh,
For wine shall bid despondence fly!
Thus—till another autumn's glow
Shall bid another vintage flow!

ODE LVII.

AND whose immortal hand could shed
Upon this disk the ocean's bed?
And, in a frenzied flight of soul
Sublime as heaven's eternal pole,

Imagine

This ode is a very animated description of a picture of Venus
on a discus, which represented the goddess in her first emer-
gence from the waves. About two centuries after our poet
wrote, the pencil of the artist Apelles embellished this subject,
in his famous painting of the Venus Anadyomené, the model
of which, as Pliny informs us, was the beautiful Campaspe,
given to him by Alexander; though, according to Natalis
Comes, lib. vii. cap. 16, it was Phryne who sat to Apelles for
the face and breast of this Venus.

There are a few blemishes in the reading of the ode before us,
which have influenced Faber, Heyne, Brunck, &c. to denounce
the whole poem as spurious. Non ego paucis offendar maculis.
I think it is beautiful enough to be authentic.

F 3

And

Imagine thus, in semblance warm,

The Queen of Love's voluptuous form

Floating along the silvery sea

In beauty's naked majesty!

Oh! he has given the captur'd sight

A witching banquet of delight;

And all those sacred scenes of love,

Where only hallow'd eyes may rove,

                                    Lie,

And whose immortal hand could shed

· *Upon this disk the ocean's bed?*] The abruptness of αφα τις τοριωσι ωσττον, is finely expressive of sudden admiration, and is one of those beauties, which we cannot but admire in their source, though, by frequent imitation, they are now become languid and unimpressive.

And all those sacred scenes of love,

Where only hallow'd eyes may rove, &c.] The picture here has all the delicate character of the semi-reducta Venus, and is the sweetest emblem· of what the poetry of passion ought to be ; glowing but through a veil, and stealing upon the heart from concealment. Few of the ancients have attained this

                                    modesty

Lie, faintly glowing, half conceal'd,

Within the lucid billows veil'd.

Light as the leaf, that summer's breeze

Has wafted o'er the glassy seas,

She floats upon the ocean's breast,

Which undulates in sleepy rest,

And stealing on, she gently pillows

Her bosom on the amorous billows.

Her bosom, like the humid rose,

Her neck, like dewy-sparkling snows,

Illume

modesty of description, which is like the golden cloud that
hung over Jupiter and Juno, impervious to every beam but that
of fancy.

Her bosom, like the humid rose, &c.] "Ροδεων (says an ano-
nymous annotator) is a whimsical epithet for the bosom."
Neither Catullus nor Gray have been of his opinion. The
former has the expression,

En hic in roseis latet papillis.

And the latter,

Lo! where the rosy-bosom'd hours, &c.

Crottus,

Illume the liquid path she traces,
And burn within the stream's embraces!
In languid luxury soft she glides,
Encircled by the azure tides,
Like some fair lily, faint with weeping,
Upon a bed of violets sleeping!
Beneath their queen's inspiring glance,
The dolphins o'er the green sea dance,
Bearing in triumph young Desire,
And baby Love with smiles of fire!

                                    While,

Crottus, a modern Latinist, might indeed be censured for
too vague an use of the epithet " rosy," when he applies it to
the eyes: " e roscis oculis."

————————*young Desire, &c.*] In the original 'Ιμερος,
who was the same deity with Jocus among the Romans. Au-
relius Augurellus has a poem beginning

        Invitat olim Bacchus ad cœnam suos
        Comon, Jocum, Cupidinem.

Which Parnell has closely imitated:

                                    Gay

While, sparkling on the silver waves,
The tenants of the briny caves
Around the pomp in eddies play,
And gleam along the watery way.

Gay Bacchus, liking Estcourt's wine,
    A noble meal bespoke us ;
And for the guests that were to dine,
    Brought Comus, Love, and Jocus, &c.

ODE LVIII.

WHEN gold, as fleet as zephyr's pinion,
Escapes like any faithless minion,
And flies me (as he flies me ever),
Do I pursue him? never, never!

No,

I have followed Barnes's arrangement of this ode; it deviates
somewhat from the Vatican MS. but it appeared to me the
more natural order.

When gold, as fleet as zephyr's pinion,

Escapes like any faithless minion, &c.] In the original
'O δραπετης ὁ χρυσος. There is a kind of pun in these words,
as Madame Dacier has already remarked; for Chrysos, which
signifies gold, was also a frequent name for a slave. In one of
Lucian's dialogues there is, I think, a similar play upon the
word, where the followers of Chrysippus are called golden
fishes. The puns of the ancients are, in general, even more
vapid than our own; some of the best are those recorded of
Diogenes.

And flies me (as he flies me ever), &c.] Αει δ', αει με φευγει.

This

No, let the false deserter go,
For who would court his direst foe?
But, when I feel my lighten'd mind
No more by ties of gold confin'd,
I loosen all my clinging cares,
And cast them to the vagrant airs.
Then, then I feel the Muse's spell,
And wake to life the dulcet shell;

This grace of iteration has already been taken notice óf.
Though sometimes merely a playful beauty, it is peculiarly
expressive of impassioned sentiment, and we may easily believe
that it was one of the many sources of that energetic sensibility
which breathed through the style of Sappho. See Gyrald. Vet.
Poet. Dial. 9. It will not be said that this is a mechanical or-
nament by any one who can feel its charm in those lines of
Catullus, where he complains of the infidelity of his mistress,
Lesbia.

> Cœli, Lesbia nostra, Lesbia illa,
> Illa Lesbia, quam Catullus unam,
> Plus quam se atque suos amavit omnes,
> Nunc, &c.

Si sic omnia dixisset! but the rest does not bear citation.

The

The dulcet shell to beauty sings,
And love dissolves along the strings!
Thus, when my heart is sweetly taught
How little gold deserves a thought,
The winged slave returns once more,
And with him wafts delicious store
Of racy wine, whose balmy art
In slumber seals the anxious heart!
Again he tries my soul to sever
From love and song, perhaps for ever!
Away, deceiver! why pursuing
Ceaseless thus my heart's undoing?
Sweet is the song of amorous fire;
Sweet are the sighs that thrill the lyre;
Oh! sweeter far than all the gold
The waftage of thy wings can hold.
I well remember all thy wiles;
They wither'd Cupid's flowery smiles,

And

And o'er his harp such garbage shed,
I thought its angel breath was fled!
They tainted all his bowl of blisses,
His bland desires and hallow'd kisses.
Oh! fly to haunts of sordid men,
But rove not near the bard again!
Thy glitter in the Muse's shade,
Scares from her bower the tuneful maid;

They tainted all his bowl of blisses,
His bland desires and hallow'd kisses.] Original:

Φιλημματων δε κεδνων,
Ποθων κυπελλα κιρνης.

Horace has " Desiderique temperare poculum," not figuratively, however, like Anacreon, but importing the love-
philtres of the witches. By " cups of kisses" our poet may
allude to a favourite gallantry among the ancients, of drinking
when the lips of their mistresses had touched the brim:

" Or leave a kiss within the cup,
And I 'll not ask for wine;"

as in Ben Jonson's translation from Philostratus; and Lucian
has a conceit upon the same idea, " Ινα και πινης αμα και
φιλης," " that you may at once both drink and kiss."

And

And not for worlds would I forego
This moment of poetic glow,
When my full soul, in Fancy's stream,
Pours o'er the lyre its swelling theme.
Away, away! to worldlings hence,
Who feel not this diviner sense,
And with thy gay, fallacious blaze,
Dazzle their unrefined gaze.

ODE LIX.

Sabled by the solar beam,
Now the fiery clusters teem,
In osier baskets, borne along
By all the festal vintage throng
Of rosy youths and virgins fair,
Ripe as the melting fruits they bear.
Now, now they press the pregnant grapes,
And now the captive stream escapes,

The title Επιληνιος ὑμνος, which Barnes has given to this
ode, is by no means appropriate. We have already had one
of those hymns (ode 56), but this is a description of the vintage; and the title εις οινον, which it bears in the Vatican MS.
is more correct than any that have been suggested.

Degen, in the true spirit of literary scepticism, doubts that
this ode is genuine, without assigning any reason for such a
suspicion. " Non amo te, Sabidi, nec possum dicere quare ;"
but this is far from satisfactory criticism.

In

In fervid tide of nectar gushing,
And for its bondage proudly blushing!
While round the vat's impurpled brim,
The choral song, the vintage hymn
Of rosy youths and virgins fair,
Steals on the cloy'd and panting air.
Mark, how they drink, with all their eyes,
The orient tide that sparkling flies;
The infant balm of all their fears,
The infant Bacchus, born in tears!
When he, whose verging years decline
As deep into the vale as mine,
When he inhales the vintage-spring,
His heart is fire, his foot 's a wing;
And as he flies, his hoary hair
Plays truant with the wanton air!
While the warm youth, whose wishing soul
Has kindled o'er the inspiring bowl,

                                    Impassion'd

Impassion'd seeks the shadowy grove,
Where, in the tempting guise of love,
Reclining sleeps some witching maid,
Whose sunny charms, but half display'd,
Blush through the bower, that, closely twin'd,
Excludes the kisses of the wind!
The virgin wakes, the glowing boy
Allures her to the embrace of joy;
Swears that the herbage heaven had spread,
Was sacred as the nuptial bed;

Swears that the herbage heaven had spread,
Was sacred as the nuptial bed; &c.] The original here has
been variously interpreted. Some, in their zeal for our author's
purity, have supposed, that the youth only persuades her to a
premature marriage. Others understand from the words
προδοτιν γαμων γιιισθαι, that he seduces her to a violation of
the nuptial vow. The turn which I have given it is somewhat
like the sentiment of Heloïsa, " amorem conjugio, libertatem
vinculo præferre." (See her original Letters.) The Italian
translations have almost all wantoned upon this description;
but that of Marchetti is indeed " nimium lubricus aspici."

That

That laws should never bind desire,
And love was nature's holiest fire!
The virgin weeps, the virgin sighs;
He kiss'd her lips, he kiss'd her eyes;
The sigh was balm, the tear was dew,
They only rais'd his flame anew.
And oh! he stole the sweetest flower
That ever bloom'd in any bower!

Such is the madness wine imparts,
Whene'er it steals on youthful hearts.

ODE LX.

Awake to life, my dulcet shell,
To Phœbus all thy sighs shall swell;
And though no glorious prize be thine,
No Pythian wreath around thee twine,
Yet every hour is glory's hour
To him who gathers wisdom's flower!

This hymn to Apollo is supposed not to have been written by Anacreon, and it certainly is rather a sublimer flight than the Teian wing is accustomed to soar. But we ought not to judge from this diversity of style, in a poet of whom time has preserved such partial relics. If we knew Horace but as a satirist, should we easily believe there could dwell such animation in his lyre? Suidas says that our poet wrote hymns, and this perhaps is one of them. We can perceive in what an altered and imperfect state his works are at present, when we find a scholiast upon Horace citing an ode from the third book of Anacreon.

Then

Then wake thee from thy magic slumbers,
Breathe to the soft and Phrygian numbers,
Which, as my trembling lips repeat,
Thy chords shall echo back as sweet.
The cygnet thus, with fading notes,
As down Cayster's tide he floats,
Plays with his snowy plumage fair
Upon the wanton murmuring air,
Which amorously lingers round,
And sighs responsive sound for sound!
Muse of the Lyre! illume my dream,
Thy Phœbus is my fancy's theme;
And hallow'd is the harp I bear,
And hallow'd is the wreath I wear,
Hallow'd by him, the god of lays,
Who modulates the choral maze!
I sing the love which Daphne twin'd
Around the godhead's yielding mind;

I sing

I sing the blushing Daphne's flight
From this æthereal youth of light;
And how the tender, timid maid
Flew panting to the kindly shade,
Resign'd a form, too tempting fair,
And grew a verdant laurel there;
Whose leaves, with sympathetic thrill,
In terror seem'd to tremble still.

And how the tender, timid maid
Flew panting to the kindly shade, &c.] Original :

> Το μὲν ἐκπεφευγε κεντρον,
> Φυσεως δ' αμειψε μορφην.

I find the word κεντρον here has a double force, as it also signifies that " omnium parentem, quam sanctus Numa, &c. &c." (See Martial.) In order to confirm this import of the word here, those who are curious in new readings, may place the stop after φυσεως, thus :

> Το μεν εκπεφευγε κεντρον
> Φυσεως; δ' αμειψε μορφην.

The

The God pursu'd, with wing'd desire;
And when his hopes were all on fire,
And when he thought to hear the sigh
With which enamour'd virgins die,
He only heard the pensive air
Whispering amid her leafy hair!
But, oh my soul! no more—no more!
Enthusiast, whither do I soar?
This sweetly-mad'ning dream of soul
Has hurried me beyond the goal.
Why should I sing the mighty darts
Which fly to wound celestial hearts,
When sure the lay, with sweeter tone,
Can tell the darts that wound my own?
Still be Anacreon, still inspire
The descant of the Teian lyre:
Still let the nectar'd numbers float,
Distilling love in every note!

                                And

And when the youth, whose burning soul
Has felt the Paphian star's control,

When

Still be Anacreon, still inspire
The descant of the Teian lyre:] The original is Τον Αναχρεοντα
μιμυ. I have translated it under the supposition that the hymn
is by Anacreon ; though I fear, from this very line, that his
claim to it can scarcely be supported.

Τον Αναχρεοντα μιμυ, "Imitate Anacreon." Such is the
lesson given us by the lyrist ; and if, in poetry, a simple elegance of sentiment, enriched by the most playful felicities of
fancy, be a charm which invites or deserves imitation, where
shall we find such a guide as Anacreon ? In morality too,
with some little reserve, I think we might not blush to follow
in his footsteps. For if his song be the language of his heart,
though luxurious and relaxed, he was artless and benevolent ;
and who would not forgive a few irregularities, when atoned
for by virtues so rare and so endearing ? When we think of the
sentiment in those lines :

> Away ! I hate the slanderous dart,
> Which steals to wound th' unwary heart,

how many are there in the world, to whom we would wish to
say, Τον Αναχρεοντα μιμυ !

Here ends the last of the odes in the Vatican MS. whose
authority confirms the genuine antiquity of them all, though a

G 3
few

When he the liquid lays shall hear,

His heart will flutter to his ear,

And drinking there of song divine,

Banquet on intellectual wine!

few have stolen among the number, which we may hesitate
in attributing to Anacreon. In the little essay prefixed to this
translation, I observed that Barnes has quoted this manuscript
incorrectly, relying upon an imperfect copy of it, which Isaac
Vossius had taken; I shall just mention two or three instances
of this inaccuracy, the first which occur to me. In the ode of
the Dove, on the words Πτεροισι συγκαλυψω, he says, "Vatican MS. συσκιαζων, etiam Prisciano invitò," though the MS.
reads συνκαλυψω, with συσκιασω interlined. Degen too, on the
same line, is somewhat in error. In the twenty-second ode of
this series, line thirteenth, the MS. has τεινη with αι interlined, and Barnes imputes to it the reading of τινδη. In the
fifty-seventh, line twelfth, he professes to have preserved the
reading of the MS. Αλαλημενη δ' επ' αυτη, while the latter has
αλαλημενος δ' επ' αυτα. Almost all the other annotators have
transplanted these errors from Barnes.

ODE LXI.

GOLDEN hues of youth are fled;
Hoary locks deform my head.
Bloomy graces, dalliance gay,
All the flowers of life decay.

Withering

The intrusion of this melancholy ode, among the careless
levities of our poet, has always reminded me of the skeletons,
which the Egyptians used to hang up in their banquet-rooms,
to inculcate a thought of mortality even amidst the dissipations
of mirth. If it were not for the beauty of its numbers, the
Teian Muse should disown this ode. Quid habet illius, illius
quæ spirabat amores?

To Stobæus we are indebted for it.

Bloomy graces, dalliance gay,

All the flowers of life decay.] Horace often, with feeling and
elegance, deplores the fugacity of human enjoyments. See
book ii. ode xi.; and thus in the second epistle, book ii.

Singula de nobis anni prædantur euntes.
Eripuere jocos, venerem, convivia, ludum.

O 4   The

Withering age begins to trace
Sad memorials o'er my face; ·
Time has shed its sweetest bloom,
All the future must be gloom ! ·
This awakes my hourly sighing;
Dreary is the thought of dying !
Pluto's is a dark abode,
Sad the journey, sad the road:

> The wing of every passing day
> Withers some blooming joy away;
> And wafts from our enamour'd arms
> The banquet's mirth, the virgin's charms.

Dreary is the thought of dying! &c.] Regnier, a libertine French poet, has written some sonnets on the approach of death, full of gloomy and trembling repentance. Chaulieu, however, supports more consistently the spirit of the Epicurean philosopher. See his poem, addressed to the Marquis La Farre,

> Plus j'approche du terme et moins je le redoute, &c.

I shall leave it to the moralist to make his reflections here: it is impossible to be very anacreontic on such a subject.

And,

And, the gloomy travel o'er,

Ah! we can return no more!

And, the gloomy travel o'er,
Ah! we can return no more!] Scaliger, upon Catullus's well-known lines, " Qui nunc it per iter, &c." remarks, that Acheron, with the same idea, is called αναξοδος by Theocritus, and δυσεκδρομος by Nicander.

ODE LXII.

Fill me, boy, as deep a draught,
As e'er was fill'd, as e'er was quaff'd;
But let the water amply flow,
To cool the grape's intemperate glow;

Let

This ode consists of two fragments, which are to be found in Athenæus, book x. and which Barnes, from the similarity of their tendency, has combined into one. I think this a very justifiable liberty, and have adopted it in some other fragments of our poet.

Degen refers us here to verses of Uz, lib. iv. der Trinker.

But let the water amply flow,

To cool the grape's intemperate glow; &c.] It was Amphictyon who first taught the Greeks to mix water with their wine; in commemoration of which circumstance they erected altars to Bacchus and the nymphs. On this mythological allegory the following epigram is founded:

Ardentem

Let not the fiery god be single,
But with the nymphs in union mingle.
For though the bowl 's the grave of sadness,
Oh ! be it ne'er the birth of madness !
No, banish from our board to-night
The revelries of rude delight !
To Scythians leave these wild excesses,
Ours be the joy that sooths and blesses !

Ardentem ex utero Semeles lavêre Lyæum
  Naiades, extincto fulminis igne sacri ;
Cum nymphis igitur trictabilis, at sine nymphis
  Candenti rursus fulmine corripitur.
                              Pierius Valeriánus.

Which is, non verbum verbo,

  While heavenly fire consum'd his Theban dame,
  A Naiad caught young Bacchus from the flame,
    And dipp'd him burning in her purest lymph ;
  Still, still he loves the sea-maid's crystal urn,
  And when his native fires infuriate burn,
    He bathes him in the fountain of the nymph.

And

And while the temperate bowl we wreathe,
Our choral hymns shall sweetly breathe,
Beguiling every hour along
With harmony of soul and song!

ODE LXIII.

To Love, the soft and blooming child,
I touch the harp in descant wild;
To Love, the babe of Cyprian bowers,
The boy, who breathes and blushes flowers!
To Love, for heaven and earth adore him,
And gods and mortals bow before him!

"This fragment is preserved in Clemens Alexandrinus, Strom.
lib. vi. and in Arsenius, Collect. Græc." Barnes.
It appears to have been the opening of a hymn in praise of
Love.

ODE LXIV.

HASTE thee, nymph, whose winged spear
Wounds the fleeting mountain-deer!
Dian, Jove's immortal child,
Huntress of the savage wild!

This hymn to Diana is extant in Hephæstion. There is an anecdote of our poet, which has led some to doubt whether he ever wrote any odes of this kind. It is related by the Scholiast upon Pindar (Isthmionic. od. ii. v. 1. as cited by Barnes). Anacreon being asked, why he addressed all his hymns to women, and none to the deities? answered, "Because women are my deities."

I have assumed the same liberty in reporting this anecdote, which I have done in translating some of the odes; and it were to be wished that these little infidelities were always considered pardonable in the interpretation of the ancients; thus, when nature is forgotten in the original, in the translation "tamen usque recurret."

Goddess

Goddess with the sun-bright hair!
Listen to a people's prayer.
Turn, to Lethe's river turn,
There thy vanquish'd people mourn!
Come to Lethe's wavy shore,
There thy people's peace restore.
Thine their hearts, their altars thine;
Dian! must they—must they pine?

Turn, to Lethe's river turn,
There thy vanquish'd people mourn!] Lethe, a river of Ionia,
according to Strabo, falling into the Meander: near to it was
situated the town Magnesia, in favour of whose inhabitants our
poet is supposed to have addressed this supplication to Diana.
It was written (as Madame Dacier conjectures) on the occasion of some battle, in which the Magnesians had been de-
feated.

ODE LXV.

Like some wanton filly sporting,
Maid of Thrace! thy fly'st my courting.
Wanton filly! tell me why
Thou trip'st away, with scornful eye,
And seem'st to think my doting heart
Is novice in the bridling art?

This ode, which is addressed to some Thracian girl, exists
in Heraclides, and has been imitated very frequently by Horace, as all the annotators have remarked. Madame Dacier
rejects the allegory, which runs so obviously throughout it,
and supposes it to have been addressed to a young mate be-
longing to Polycrates: there is more modesty than ingenuity in
the lady's conjecture.

Pierius, in the fourth book of his Hieroglyphics, cites this
ode, and informs us, that a horse was the hieroglyphical emblem of pride.

                                    Believe

Believe me, girl, it is not so ;
Thou 'lt find this skilful hand can throw
The reins upon that tender form,
However wild, however warm !
Thou 'lt own that I can tame thy force,
And turn and wind thee in the course.
Though wasting now thy careless hours,
Thou sport amid the herbs and flowers,
Thou soon shalt feel the rein's control,
And tremble at the wish'd-for goal !

Turn to Myrilla, turn thine eye,
Breathe to Myrilla, breathe thy sigh!
To those bewitching beauties turn;
For thee they mantle, flush, and burn!
Not more the rose, the queen of flowers,
Outblushes all the glow of bowers,
Then she unrivall'd bloom discloses,
The sweetest rose, where all are roses!
Oh! may the sun, benignant, shed
His blandest influence o'er thy bed;
And foster there an infant tree,
To blush like her, and bloom like thee!

And foster there an infant tree,
To blush like her, and bloom like thee] Original Κυπαρισσος δε τιφυκοι σιυ ινι κππω. Passeratius, upon the words "cum castum amisit florem," in the nuptial song of Catullus, after explaining "flos" in somewhat a similar sense to that which Gaulminus attributes to ροδον, says, "Hortum quoque vocant in quo flos ille carpitur, et Græcis κηπον ισι το σφηξαιον γυναικων."

May

May I remark, that the author of the Greek version of this charming ode of Catullus, has neglected a most striking and Anacreontic beauty in those verses " Ut flos in septis, &c." which is the repetition of the line, " Multi illum pueri, multæ optavêre puellæ," with the slight alteration of nulli and nullæ. Catullus himself, however, has been equally injudicious in his version of the famous ode of Sappho ; he has translated γιλωσας ἱμιρον, but takes no notice of ἡδυ φωνεισας. Horace has caught the spirit of it more faithfully :

> Dulce ridentem Lalagen amabo
> Dulce loquentem.

ODE LXVII.

GENTLE youth! whose looks assume
Such a soft and girlish bloom,
Why, repulsive, why refuse
The friendship which my heart pursues?
Thou little know'st the fond control
With which thy virtue reins my soul!
Then smile not on my locks of grey;
Believe me, oft with converse gay,

I have formed this poem of three or four different fragments, which is a liberty that perhaps may be justified by the example of Barnes, who has thus compiled the fifty-seventh of his edition, and the little ode beginning φιρ' ύδας, φιρ' οινον, ω παι, which he has subjoined to the epigrams.

The fragments combined in this ode, are the sixty-seventh, ninety-sixth, ninety-seventh, and hundredth of Barnes's edition, to which I refer the reader for the names of the authors by whom they are preserved.

I've

I 've chain'd the ears of tender age,
And boys have lov'd the prattling sage !
For mine is many a soothing pleasure,
And mine is many a soothing measure ;
And much I hate the beamless mind,
Whose earthly vision, unrefin'd,
Nature has never form'd to see
The beauties of simplicity !
Simplicity, the flower of heaven,
To souls elect, by nature given !

And boys have lov'd the prattling sage !] Monsieur Chaulieu
has given a very amiable idea of an old man's intercourse with
youth :

> Que cherche par les jeunes gens,
> Pour leurs erreurs plein d'indulgence,
> Je tolere leur imprudence
> En faveur de leurs agrémens.

H 4

ODE LXVIII.

Rich in bliss, I proudly scorn
The stream of Amalthea's horn!
Nor should I ask to call the throne
Of the Tartessian prince my own;
To totter through his train of years,
The victim of declining fears.
One little hour of joy to me
Is worth a dull eternity!

This fragment is preserved in the third book of Strabo.

Of the Tartessian prince my own;] He here alludes to Arganthonius, who lived, according to Lucian, an hundred and fifty years; and reigned, according to Herodotus, eighty. See Barnes.

ODE LXIX.

Now Neptune's sullen month appears,
The angry night-cloud swells with tears ;
And savage storms, infuriate driven,
Fly howling in the face of heaven!
Now, now, my friends, the gathering gloom
With roseate rays of wine illume:
And while our wreaths of parsley spread
Their fadeless foliage round our head,
We 'll hymn th' almighty power of wine,
And shed libations on his shrine!

This is composed of two fragments; the seventieth and
eighty-first in Barnes. They are both found in Eustathius.

ODE LXX.

THEY wove the lotus band to deck,
And fan with pensile wreath their neck ;
And every guest, to shade his head,
Three little breathing chaplets spread;

Three fragments form this little ode, all of which are preserved in Athenæus. They are the eighty-second, seventy-
fifth, and eighty-third, in Barnes.

And every guest, to shade his head,
Three little breathing chaplets spread ;] Longepierre, to give
an idea of the luxurious estimation in which garlands were held
by the ancients, relates an anecdote of a courtezan, who, in
order to gratify three lovers, without leaving cause for jealousy
with any of them, gave a kiss to one, let the other drink after
her, and put a garland on the brow of the third ; so that each
was satisfied with his favour, and flattered himself with the pre-
ference.

This circumstance is extremely like the subject of one of the
tensons of Savari de Mauléon, a troubadour. See L'Histoire
Littéraire des Troubadours. The recital is a curious picture of
the puerile gallantries of chivalry.

And

And one was of Egyptian leaf,
The rest were roses, fair and brief!
While from a golden vase profound,
To all on flowery beds around,
A goblet-nymph, of heavenly shape,
Pour'd the rich weepings of the grape!

ODE LXXI.

A BROKEN cake, with honey sweet,
Is all my spare and simple treat:
And while a generous bowl I crown
To float my little banquet down,
I take the soft, the amorous lyre,
And sing of love's delicious fire!
In mirthful measures, warm and free,
I sing, dear maid, and sing for thee!

This poem is compiled by Barnes, from Athenæus, Hephæstion, and Arsenius. See Barnes, 80th.

ODE LXXII.

WITH twenty chords my lyre is hung,
  And while I wake them all for thee,
Thou, O virgin, wild and young,
  Disport'st in airy levity.

The nursling fawn, that in some shade
  Its antler'd mother leaves behind,
Is not more wantonly afraid,
  More timid of the rustling wind!

This I have formed from the eighty-fourth and eighty-fifth
of Barnes's edition. The two fragments are found in Athenæus.

The nursling fawn, that in some shade
  Its antler'd mother leaves behind, &c.]   In the original:

      ʽΟς εν ὑλη κεροεσσης
      Απολιφθεις ὑπο μητρος.

                              "Horned"

"Horned" here, undoubtedly, seems a strange epithet; Madam Dacier however observes, that Sophocles, Callimachus, &c. have all applied it in the very same manner, and she seems to agree in the conjecture of the Scholiast upon Pindar, that perhaps horns are not always peculiar to the males. I think we may with more ease conclude it to be a license of the poet, "jussit habere puellam cornua."

ODE LXXIII.

FARE thee well, perfidious maid!
My soul, too long on earth delay'd,
Delay'd, perfidious girl! by thee,
Is now on wing for liberty.
I fly to seek a kindlier sphere,
Since thou hast ceas'd to love me here!

This fragment is preserved by the Scholiast upon Aristophanes, and is the eighty-seventh in Barnes.

ODE LXXIV.

I BLOOM'D awhile, an happy flower,
Till love approach'd one fatal hour,
And made my tender branches feel
The wounds of his avenging steel.
Then, then I feel, like some poor willow
That tosses on the wintry billow!

This is to be found in Hephæstion, and is the eighty-ninth
of Barnes's edition.

I must here apologize for omitting a very considerable fragment imputed to our poet, Ξανθη δ' Ευρυπυλη μελει, &c. which
is preserved in the twelfth book of Athenæus, and is the ninety-
first in Barnes. If it was really Anacreon who wrote it, nil
fuit unquam sic impar sibi. It is in a style of gross satire, and
is full of expressions which never could be gracefully translated.

ODE LXXV.

Monarch Love! resistless boy,
With whom the rosy Queen of Joy,
And nymphs, that glance ethereal blue,
Disporting tread the mountain-dew;
Propitious, oh! receive my sighs,
Which, burning with entreaty, rise,
That thou wilt whisper to the breast
Of her I love thy soft behest;
And counsel her to learn from thee
The lesson thou hast taught to me.
Ah! if my heart no flattery tell,
Thou 'lt own I 've learn'd that lesson well!

This fragment is preserved by Dion Chrysostom. Orat. ii. de
Regno. See Barnes, 93.

ODE LXXVI.

Spirit of Love, whose tresses shine
Along the breeze, in golden twine;
Come, within a fragrant cloud,
Blushing with light, thy votary shroud;

And,

This fragment, which is extant in Athenæus (Barnes, 101),
is supposed, on the authority of Chamæleon, to have been addressed to Sappho. We have also a stanza attributed to her,
which some romancers have supposed to be her answer to
Anacreon. "Mais par malheur (as Bayle says), Sappho vint
au monde environ cent ou six vingt ans avant Anacreon."
Nouvelles de la Rép. des Lett. tom. ii. de Novembre 1684. The
following is her fragment, the compliment of which is very
finely imagined; she supposes that the Muse has dictated the
verses of Anacreon:

Κεινον, ω χρυσοθρονι Μυσ' ενιστες
'Υμνον, εκ της καλλιγυναικος εσθλαυ
Τηιος χωρας ὁν αειδι τερπνως
Πρεσβυς αγανος.

Oh

And, on those wings that sparkling play,
Waft, oh! waft me hence away!
Love! my soul is full of thee,
Alive to all thy luxury.
But she, the nymph for whom I glow,
The pretty Lesbian, mocks my woe;
Smiles at the hoar and silver'd hues
Which Time upon my forehead strews.
Alas! I fear she keeps her charms,
In store for younger, happier arms!

Oh Muse! who sitt'st on golden throne,
Full many a hymn of dulcet tone
  The Teian sage is taught by thee;
But, Goddess, from thy throne of gold,
The sweetest hymn thou 'st ever told,
  He lately learn'd and sang for me.

ODE LXXVII.

Hither, gentle Muse of mine,
  Come and teach thy votary old,
Many a golden hymn divine,
  For the nymph with vest of gold.

Pretty nymph, of tender age,
  Fair thy silky locks unfold;
Listen to a hoary sage,
  Sweetest maid with vest of gold!

*

This is formed of the 124th and 119th fragments in Barnes, both of which are to be found in Scaliger's Poetics.

De Pauw thinks that those detached lines and couplets, which Scaliger has adduced as examples in his Poetics, are by no means authentic, but of his own fabrication.

ODE LXXVIII.

Would that I were a tuneful lyre,
 Of burnish'd ivory fair;
Which, in the Dionysian choir,
 Some blooming boy should bear!

Would that I were a golden vase,
 And then some nymph should hold
My spotless frame, with blushing grace,
 Herself as pure as gold!

This is generally inserted among the remains of Alcæus.
Some, however, have attributed it to Anacreon. See our poet's
twenty-second ode, and the notes.

ODE LXXIX.

WHEN Cupid sees my beard of snow,
Which blanching Time has taught to flow,
Upon his wing of golden light
He passes with an eaglet's flight,
And flitting on he seems to say,
" Fare thee well, thou 'st had thy day !"

See Barnes, 173d. This fragment, to which I have taken
the liberty of adding a turn, not to be found in the original, is
cited by Lucian, in his little essay on the Gallic Hercules.

Cupid, whose lamp has lent the ray,
Which lightens our meandering way;
Cupid, within my bosom stealing,
Excites a strange and mingled feeling,
Which pleases, though severely teasing,
And teases, though divinely pleasing!

Barnes, 125th.   This, if I remember right, is in Scaliger's
Poetics.   Gail has omitted it in his collection of fragments.

I 4

LET me resign a wretched breath,
  Since now remains to me
No other balm than kindly death
  To soothe my misery!

This fragment is extant in Arsenius and Hephæstion. See
Barnes (69th), who has arranged the metre of it very elegantly.

I KNOW thou lov'st a brimming measure,
　And art a kindly, cordial host;
But let me fill and drink at pleasure,
　Thus I enjoy the goblet most.

Barnes, 72d. This fragment, which is quoted by Athenæus.
is an excellent lesson for the votaries of Jupiter Hospitalis.

I FEAR that love disturbs my rest,
    Yet feel not love's impassion'd care ;
I think there's madness in my breast,
    Yet cannot find that madness there !

This fragment is in Hephæstion. See Barnes, 95th.
Catullus expresses something of this contrariety of feelings :

  Odi et amo ; quare id faciam fortasse requiris ;
    Nescio: sed fieri sentio, et excrucior. Carm. 53.

I love thee and hate thee, but if I can tell
  The cause of my love and my hate, may I die !
I can feel it, alas ! I can feel it too well,
  That I love thee and hate thee, but cannot tell why.

FROM dread Leucadia's frowning steep,
I'll plunge into the whitening deep :
And there I'll float to waves resign'd,
For Love intoxicates my mind !

This also is in Hephæstion, and perhaps is a fragment of some poem, in which Anacreon had commemorated the fate of Sappho. It is the 123d of Barnes.

MIX me, child, a cup divine,
Crystal water, ruby wine :
Weave the frontlet, richly flushing,
O'er my wintry temples blushing.
Mix the brimmer—Love and I
Shall no more the gauntlet try.
Here—upon this holy bowl,
I surrender all my soul !

This fragment is collected by Barnes from Demetrius Phale-
reus, and Eustathius, and is subjoined in his edition to the
epigrams attributed to our poet. And here is the last of those
little scattered flowers, which I thought I might venture with
any grace to transplant. I wish it could be said of the garland
which they form, To δ' ω̃ Ασαριοττος.

Among the Epigrams of the Anthologia, there are some panegyrics on Anacreon, which I had translated, and originally intended as a kind of Coronis to the work; but I found, upon consideration, that they wanted variety; a frequent recurrence of the same thought, within the limits of an epitaph, to which they are confined, would render a collection of them rather uninteresting. I shall take the liberty, however, of subjoining a few, that I may not appear to have totally neglected those elegant tributes to the reputation of Anacreon. The four epigrams which I give are imputed to Antipater Sidonius. They are rendered, perhaps, with too much freedom; but designing a translation of all that are on the subject, I imagined it was necessary to enliven their uniformity by sometimes indulging in the liberties of paraphrase.

Αντιπατρα Σιδωνια, εις Ανακρεοντα.

ΘΑΛΛΟΙ τετρακορυμβος, Ανακρεον, αμφι σε κισσος
αβρα τε λειμωνων πορφυριων πεταλα·
πηγαι δ' αργινοεντος αναθλιβοιντο γαλακτος,
ευωδες δ' απο γης ήδυ χιοιτο μεθυ,
οφρα κι τοι σποδιη τε και οςεα τερψιν αρηται,
ει δε τις φθιμενοις χρεμπτεται ευφροσυνα,
ω το φιλον ςερξας, φιλε, βαρβιτον, ω συν αοιδα
παντα διαπλωσας και συν ερωτι βιον.

Around the tomb, oh bard divine!
  Where soft thy hallow'd brow reposes,
Long may the deathless ivy twine,
  And summer pour her waste of roses!

And many a fount shall there distil,
  And many a rill refresh the flowers;
But wine shall gush in every rill,
  And every fount be milky showers.

Thus,

Thus, shade of him, whom Nature taught
To tune his lyre and soul to pleasure,
Who gave to love his warmest thought,
Who gave to love his fondest measure!

Thus, after death, if spirits feel,
Thou may'st, from odours round thee stream-
ing,
A pulse of past enjoyment steal,
And live again in blissful dreaming!

Antipater Sidonius, the author of this epigram, lived, according to Vossius, de Poetis Græcis, in the second year of the
169th Olympiad. He appears, from what Cicero and Quin-
tilian have said of him, to have been a kind of improvvisatore.
See Institut. Orat. lib. x. cap. 7. There is nothing more
known respecting this poet, except some particulars about his
illness and death, which are mentioned as curious by Pliny and
others; and there remain of his works but a few epigrams in
the Anthologia, among which are these I have selected, upon
Anacreon. Those remains have been sometimes imputed to
another

another poet * of the same name, of whom Vossius gives us the
following account: " Antipater Thessalonicensis vixit tem-
pore Augusti Cæsaris, ut qui saltantem viderit Pyladem, sicut
constat ex quodam ejus epigrammate Ανθολογιας, lib. iv. tit.
ωε ορχηςριδαι.   At eum ac Bathyllum primos fuisse pantomimos
ac sub Augusto claruisse, satis notum ex Dione, &c. &c."

The reader, who thinks it worth observing, may find a
strange oversight in Hoffman's quotation of this article from
Vossius, Lexic. Univers.   By the omission of a sentence he has
made Vossius assert that the poet Antipater was one of the first
pantomime dancers in Rome.

Barnes, upon the epigram before us, mentions a version of
it by Brodæus, which is not to be found in that commentator ;
but he more than once confounds Brodæus, with another annotator on the Anthologia, Vincentius Obsopœus, who has given
a translation of the epigram.

* Pleraque tamen Thessalonicensi tribuenda videntur.
                              Brunck, Lectiones et Emendat.

Τις αυλω, κις τον αυλον.

ΤΥΜΒΟΣ Ανακριωνος. ὁ Τηιος ινθαδι κυκνος
  Ευδει, χη ανωιδων ζωροταιη μανιη.
Ακμην λιμροιση μιλιζιlαι αμφι Βαθυλλω
  Ἱμιρα· και κισση λιυκος οδωδι λιθος.
Ουδ' Αιδης σοι ιρωlας απισ6ισιν· εν δ' Αχιροίος
  Ων, ὁλος ωδινεις Κυπριδι θιρμοlιρη.

H ERE sleeps Anacreon, in this ivied shade;
Here mute in death the Teian swan is laid.
Cold, cold the heart, which liv'd but to respire
All the voluptuous frenzy of desire!

                                        And

―――― *the Teian swan is laid.*] Thus Horace of Pindar :

  Multa Dircæum levat aura cycnum.

A swan was the hieroglyphical emblem of a poet. Anacreon
has been called the swan of Teos by another of his eulogists.

And yet, oh Bard! thou art not mute in death,
Still, still we catch thy lyre's delicious breath;
And still thy songs of soft Bathylla bloom,
Green as the ivy round the mouldering tomb!

Nor

Εν τοις μελιχροις 'Ιμεροισι συνζοφος
Λυαι@- Ανακριονζα, Τηιον κυκνον,
Εσφαλας ὑγρη σικταρ@- μελυδονη.
Ευγετυς, Ανθολογ.

God of the grape! thou hast betray'd
In wine's bewildering dream,
The fairest swan that ever play'd
Along the Muses' stream!
The Teian, nurs'd with all those honied boys
The young Desires, light Loves, and rose-lip'd Joys!

Still, still we catch thy lyre's delicious breath;] Thus Simonides, speaking of our poet:

Μολπης δ' ε ληθη μελιτερπι@- αλλ' ετι κεινο
Βαρβιτον εδε θανων ευτασεν εν αιδη.
Σιμωνιδε, Ανθολογ.

Nor yet are all his numbers mute,
Though dark within the tomb he lies;
But living still, his amorous lute
With sleepless animation sighs!

This

Nor yet has death obscur'd thy fire of love,
Still, still it lights thee through th' Elysian grove ;
And dreams are thine, that bless th' elect alone,
And Venus calls thee ev'n in death her own!

This is the famous Simonides, whom Plato styled " divine ;"
though Le Fevre, in his Poëtes Grecs, supposes that the epigrams under his name are all falsely imputed. The most considerable of his remains is a satirical poem upon women, preserved by Stobæus, Ψογ⊙ γυναικων.

We may judge from the lines I have just quoted, and the
import of the epigram before us, that the works of Anacreon
were perfect in the times of Simonides and Antipater. Obsopœus, the commentator here, appears to exult in their de-
struction, and telling us they were burned by the bishops and
patriarchs, he adds, " nec sane id necquicquam fecerunt,"
attributing to this outrage an effect which it could never pro-
duce.

Τε αυλε, εις τον αυλον.

ΜΕΙΝΕ, ταφον παρα λιτον Ανακρειοντος αμειβων,
   Ει τι τοι εκ βιβλων ηλθεν εμων οφελος,
Σπεισον εμη σποδιη, σπεισον γανος, οφρα κεν οινω
   Οστεα γηθησι ταμα νοτιζομενα,
Ὡς ὁ Διονυσε μεμελημενος νασι κωμος,
   Ὡς ὁ φιλακρητε συντροφος ἁρμονιης,
Μηδε καταφθιμενος Βακχε διχα τουτον ὑποισω
   Τον γενεη μεροπων χωρον οφειλομενον.

Oн stranger! if Anacreon's shell
Has ever taught thy heart to swell
With passion's throb or pleasure's sigh,
In pity turn, as wandering nigh,

                                                    And

The spirit of Anacreon utters these verses from the tomb,
somewhat "mutatus ab illo," at least in simplicity of expression.

                                        2

And drop thy goblet's richest tear
In exquisite libation here!

So

——*if Anacreon's shell*
Has ever taught thy heart to swell, &c.] We may guess from
the words εκ βιβλων εμων, that Anacreon was not merely a writer
of billets-doux, as some French critics have called him.
Amongst these Mr. Le Fevre, with all his professed admiration,
has given our poet a character by no means of an elevated cast :

> Aussi c'est pour cela que la postérité
> L'a toujours justement d'age en age chanté
> Comme un franc goguenard, ami de goinfrerie,
> Ami de billets-doux et de badinerie.

See the verses prefixed to his Poëtes Grecs. This is unlike
the language of Theocritus, to whom Anacreon is indebted for
the following simple eulogium :

Εις Ανακρεοντ⊙ ανδριαντα.

Θασαι τον ανδριαντα τουτον, ω ξενε,
σπευδα, και λεγ', οπην αν οικον ενθης
Ανακρεοντος εικον' ειδον εν Τεω.
των προσθ' ει τι περισσον ωδοποιων
προσθεις δε χ'ωτι τοις νεοισιν αδιλο,
ερεις απρεκεως ολον τον ανδρα.

K 3

Upon

So shall my sleeping ashes thrill

With visions of enjoyment still.

I cannot ev'n in death resign

The festal joys that once were mine,

Upon the Statue of Anacreon.

Stranger! who near this statue chance to roam,

   Let it awhile your studious eyes engage;

And you may say, returning to your home,

    " I 've seen the image of the Teian sage,

   Best of the bards who deck the Muse's page."

Then, if you add, " That striplings lov'd him well,"

You tell them all he was, and aptly tell.

The simplicity of this inscription has always delighted me; I have given it, I believe, as literally as a verse translation will allow.

And drop thy goblet's richest tear, &c.] Thus Simonides, in another of his epitaphs on our poet:

   Και μιν αει τεγγοι νοτιρη δροσω, ης ο γεραιω

   Λαροτερον μαλακων εισιεν εκ στομαΐων.

   Let vines, in clustering beauty wreath'd,

    Drop all their treasures on his head,

   Whose lips a dew of sweetness breath'd,

    Richer than vine hath ever shed!

                                When

When Harmony pursu'd my ways,
And Bacchus wanton'd to my lays.
Oh! if delight could charm no more,
If all the goblet's bliss were o'er,
When fate had once our doom decreed,
Then dying would be death indeed!
Nor could I think, unblest by wine,
Divinity itself divine!

And Bacchus wanton'd to my lays, &c.] The original here is corrupted; the line ἐι ὁ Διονυσου, &c. is unintelligible.

Brunck's emendation improves the sense, but I doubt if it can be commended for elegance. He reads the line thus:

ἐι ὁ Διονυσοιο λελασμεν Θ· υπολι κυμαιτ·

See Brunck, Analecta Veter. Poet. Græc. vol. ii.

Τα αυΊα, εις τον αυΊον.

ΕΥΔΕΙΣ εν Φθιμενοισιν, Ανάκρεον, εσθλα ποησας
ευδει δ' η γλυκερη πηκλελαλος κιθαρα,
ευδει και Σμερδις, το Ποθων εαρ, ω συ μελισδων
βαρβιτ', ανεκρυη νεκΊαρ εναρμονιον.
ευδεις γαρ Ερωτος εφυς σκοπος· ες δε σε μηνη
τοξα τι και σκολιας ειχεν επιβολιας.

At length thy golden hours have wing'd their
    flight,
And drowsy death that eyelid steepeth;
Thy harp, that whisper'd through each lingering
    night,
Now mutely in oblivion sleepeth!

                                        She

Thy harp, that whisper'd through each lingering night, &c.] In
another of these poems, "the nightly-speaking lyre" of the
bard is not allowed to be silent even after his death.

She too, for whom that harp profusely shed
The purest nectar of its numbers,
She, the young spring of thy desires, has fled,
And with her blest Anacreon slumbers!

Farewell!

αις ὁ φιλακρητ⊙ τε και φιλοσοφης φιλοπαιμ⊙
παννυχι⊙ κρωοι* των φιλοπαιδα χελιν.

Σιμωνιδε, εις Ανακρεονία.

To beauty's smile and wine's delight,
To joys he lov'd on earth so well,
Still shall his spirit all the night
Attune the wild, aërial shell!

She, the young spring of thy desires, &c.] The original, το Ποθων
εαρ, is beautiful. We regret that such praise should be lavished
so preposterously, and feel that the poet's mistress Eurypyle
would have deserved it better. Her name has been told us by
Meleager, as already quoted, and in another epigram by Antipater.

υγρα δε δερχομενοισιν εν ομμασιν αλον αιδοιε,
αιδυσσων λιπαρες ανθ⊙ υπερθι κομης,
τι αρ⊙ Ευρυπυλην πιτραμμενος . . . .

* Brunck has κρωων; but κρωοι, the common reading, better
suits a detached quotation.

Long

Farewell! thou hadst a pulse for every dart
That Love could scatter from his quiver;
And every woman found in thee a heart,
Which thou, with all thy soul, didst give her!

Long may the nymph around thee play,
Eurypyle, thy soul's desire!
Basking her beauties in the ray
That lights thine eyes' dissolving fire!

Sing of her smile's bewitching power,
Her every grace that warms and blesses;
Sing of her brow's luxuriant flower,
The beaming glory of her tresses.

The expression here, ανθ- κομης, "the flower of the hair,"
is borrowed from Anacreon himself, as appears by a fragment
of the poet preserved in Stobæus: Ανικυρας δ' αναλοι αμωμιτο
ανθ-.

The purest nectar of its numbers, &c.]   Thus, says Brunck, in
the prologue to the Satires of Persius:

Cantare credas Pegaseium nectar.

"Melos"

"Melos" is the usual reading in this line, and Casaubon has
defended it; but "nectar," I think, is much more spirited.

Farewell! thou hadst a pulse for every dart, &c.] ———,
"scopus eras naturâ," not "speculator," as Barnes very falsely
interprets it.

Vincentius Obsopœus, upon this passage, contrives to indulge
us with a little astrological wisdom, and talks in a style of
learned scandal about Venus, "male posita cum Marte in domo
Saturni."

And every woman found in thee a heart, &c.] This couplet is
not otherwise warranted by the original, than as it dilates the
thought which Antipater has figuratively expressed.

Critias, of Athens, pays a tribute to the legitimate gallantry
of Anacreon, calling him, with elegant conciseness, γυναικων
πειροτευμα.

> Τον δε γυναικειων μιλεων πλεξαντα ποτ' ωδας,
> Ἡδυν Ανακρειοντα *, Τεως εις Ἑλλαδ' ανηγεν,
> Συμποσιων ερεθισμα,' γυναικων πειροτευμα.

> Teos gave to Greece her treasure,
> Sage Anacreon, sage in loving;
> Fondly weaving lays of pleasure
> For the maids who blush'd approving!

* Thus Scaliger, in his dedicatory verses to Ronsard:
Blandus, suaviloquus, dulcis Anacreon.

Oh!

Oh! in nightly banquets sporting,
    Where's the guest could ever fly him?
Oh! with love's seduction courting,
    Where's the nymph could e'er deny him?

INDEX.

VOL. I.